I0527930

Our Story of the God of Miracles

Michael and Kim Davis

Copyright © 2024 by Michael and Kim Davis

All rights reserved. No part of this publication may be reproduced, distributed, or transmitted in any form without the prior written permission of the author, except in the case of brief quotations embodied in critical reviews and certain other noncommercial uses permitted by copyright law.

For permissions requests, write to the author at:
davisworldmissions@gmail.com

ISBN: 979-8-9878969-7-6

Scripture quotations marked TPT are from The Passion Translation (C). Copyright (C) 2017, 2018, 2020 by Passion & Fire Ministries, Inc. Used by permission. All rights reserved. ThePassionTranslation.com.

Scripture quotations taken from THE AMPLIFIED BIBLE, Copyright (C) 1954, 1958, 1962, 1964,1965, 1987 by the Lockman Foundation. All rights reserved. Used by permission. (www.Lockman.org)

Scripture quotations marked NKJV are taken from The Holy Bible, New King James Version. Copyright (C) 1982 by Thomas Nelson, Inc.

Scripture quotations taken from The Holy Bible, New International Version (C) NIV (C) Copyright (C) 1973, 1978, 1984, 2011 by Biblica, Inc. TM Used by permission. All rights reserved worldwide.

Scripture quotations marked NLT are taken from the Holy Bible, New Living Translation, copyright (C) 1996, 2004, 2007 by Tyndale House Foundation. Used by permission of Tyndale House Publishers, Inc., Carol Stream, Illinois 60188. All rights reserved.

Scripture quotations from THE MESSAGE. Copyright © by Eugene H. Peterson 1993, 2002, 2005, 2018. Used by permission of NavPress. All rights reserved. Represented by Tyndale House Publishers, Inc.

Self-Publishing Services by: Antioch Books
antiochbookspublishing.com

Table of Contents

PREFACE

Over the past 35 years, God has taken us on an amazing journey, sending us from Maine to Mexico as His ambassadors with the message of the Gospel. We have seen Him do miracle after miracle, demonstrating His great love and transforming the lives of so many who have been touched by His outstretched hand.

The purpose of this book is twofold. First, we want it to inspire your faith and take it to another level. Genuine faith in the living God—the God who created Heaven and Earth—the kind of faith that believes He can do anything. So how do you get that kind of faith? How do you turn what you're hoping for into a rock-solid faith that reaches out and takes hold of what you're believing for?

The Bible is full of stories of people hearing about the miracles that Jesus did for others. As a result, faith was born in their hearts and created a miracle in their own life. For instance, when the woman with the issue of blood who was sick for twelve years heard of the miracles that Jesus did, she said, "If I may touch but his clothes, I shall be whole," (Mark 5:28 KJV).

Faith came alive in her and propelled her to find this Jesus who was going about doing good and healing all who were sick and oppressed by the devil. She found herself going out into the crowd that was thronging Jesus, and she pushed her way through until she touched Jesus' clothes and was instantly made whole. Her faith found her miracle!

The stories you are about to read are miracles that Jesus has done in our own personal lives and the lives that have been touched by the power of the Gospel message of Jesus Christ. Our prayer is that your faith will also suddenly come alive and be transformed from hope in the living God to a miracle-producing faith in your life.

The second reason for writing this book is to invite you to help us continue building the kingdom of God as we spread the Good News of the Gospel and plant and build many more churches for the glory of God.

You will read the testimonies of how God has raised up pastors and transformed their lives from being alcoholics or musicians who played in bars or someone who was born in a mountain village and whose father was brutally murdered in their infancy, but God had an amazing plan for their lives. He took them out of a life of obscurity in a remote village into a life of pastoring churches in a cartel-dominated city for the past ten years.

In 1982, the Lord sent us to Maine to plant a church with two other couples, and seven years later it was a thriving church that hosted pastor's conferences for the state of Maine. We invited speakers including Charles Cowen, Bob Yandian, Jonathan Del Turco, Richard Meyers, and many more. We were content living in the beautiful state of Maine, co-pastoring New Life Family Church when God asked us to move to Mexico with our two young children to pastor churches that had just been planted after a whirlwind crusade and medical clinics.

On that trip, we saw hundreds come to Christ, and God healed a partially paralyzed little girl in one of the medical clinics when a prayer team prayed for her healing. You will read her story of how God not only healed her but rocked the village she was living in as her mother testified about the power of God to all of her friends and relatives. Just like in the book of Acts, you will read stories of miracles one right after another.

We have a mandate to not only preach the Good News of the Gospel but to demonstrate the power of the Gospel through prayer and planting and building new churches. Over the past thirty-five years, we have watched God transform lives, heal the sick, and set the captives free. And as a result, new churches were birthed. We have built seven churches and we have a one-year Bible Institute, Revelation.

God is a God of miracles, and as you read through the pages of this book, you will encounter the various stories of the miracles He has performed in our own lives and in the lives of many different individuals that our ministry has touched over the years. God is a good God, and He has demonstrated His desire to heal the sick over and over again.

God is love, and every good and wonderful gift comes down from the Father of lights! God's radiant love will shine brighter and brighter as you read through the stories of God's miracles in the pages ahead. Jesus has left His footprints throughout Mexico by the miracles He has performed. What an honor it is to serve such a loving Savior!

Jesus is the same yesterday, today, and forever! What He did then, He is still doing today. His love for mankind has never changed. If anything, it is growing even stronger. Our prayer for you is that His immense love will spill over into your heart as you read these stories and personally encounter the God of miracles!

MIRACLES AND MISSIONS

Mama, Your Daughter Can Walk!

But Peter said, 'I don't have any silver or gold for you. But I'll give you what I have. In the name of Jesus Christ the Nazarene, get up and walk!' Then Peter took the lame man by the right hand and helped him up. And as he did, the man's feet and ankles were instantly healed and strengthened. He jumped up, stood on his feet, and began to walk! Then, walking, leaping, and praising God, he went into the Temple with them.
— Acts 3:6-8 NLT

Kim and I were co-pastors of New Life Family Church in Portland, Maine, when we were invited on a medical mission trip to share the Gospel with the impoverished villages in the Yucatán Peninsula just outside Cancun, Mexico. We were stunned when we saw the level of poverty these people were living in. Their houses were tiny, consisted of just one room, and had dirt floors. The corner posts on their houses were made from tree limbs, and the walls were made of the stems of palm branches nailed to the wood posts. The roof was corrugated tar paper nailed to sticks cut from palm trees.

As I went around inviting people to the free medical clinics, some invited me into their homes. I noticed that there were no beds—just pieces of cardboard lying on the dirt floor for them to sleep on. Sometimes there would be a hammock hanging from wood posts they had put up. Occasionally, I would see a table and a few chairs but nothing else. There weren't any bathrooms or kitchens or any walls that separated into different rooms.

Meanwhile, Kim was working in the pharmacy part of the mission, separating the medications to hand out after the people had their doctor's visit. After seeing the doctor, everyone passed through the prayer clinic, where the prayer team shared the Gospel message and offered prayer for healing. After prayer, they would receive their medications.

A mother came through the clinic with three of her children.

Her five-year-old daughter was paralyzed on her left side. The prayer team quickly went to work praying for God to heal this little girl. The team erupted in shouts of praise as the little girl suddenly was able to raise her left arm.

The leader of the prayer team noticed that the expression on the mother's face hadn't changed at all; she was still looking downcast. When they asked her why, she said, "She still can't walk." She was right. The prayer team got back to praying for the young girl, and in moments, the little girl ran to Mama! Now the team really was shouting, and Mama was overcome with joy!

The next day, the Governor's wife was holding a grand opening for a new kindergarten facility, and this same mother was there with her children. One of the full-time missionaries who lived there and was part of our group was walking by the facility, and the mother saw him. She quickly grabbed him and pushed him toward where the Governor's wife was standing.

She interrupted the event and said, "You need to give this American some land with a building so they can have a medical clinic here. I took my daughter to your clinic last year and they said they couldn't do anything to help her. Yesterday I took my daughter to their clinic, and look at her! She can walk, move her arm, and play with the other children!"

Surprised and visibly upset, the Governor's wife quickly turned and looked at the missionary and asked, "Who are you and what are you doing in my village?" The missionary explained that we were holding free medical clinics and had secured permission to hold these events. Instead of being happy for the woman and her daughter, she became angry and made a call on her phone.

Shortly after her call, the clinic was surrounded by six military Humvees filled with soldiers, all armed with machine guns! They watched us intently as we continued with the medical clinics. We passed the word around for everyone to pray and just continue doing what we were doing before and show no signs of fear or intimidation.

We had clowns as entertainment for the children at our clinics. They were part of our group, and we had them continue to walk around and hand out candy and continue their humorous skits for the children—business as usual. After just a few hours, the military packed up and left!

That night, we held an open-air crusade with generators and lights, along with a music group playing and singing praises to God. There was no electricity in this village, and it was normally pitch black at night. But that night, the village was lit up and alive with praise. The whole village came out for the event, so hundreds of people were in attendance.

The director of the missions organization invited me to preach the message that night, so I preached: "Jesus is the same yesterday, today, and forever! What He did in the Gospels, He is still doing today!" After the message, I invited them to come forward for healing and salvation, and the majority that were there that night came forward to receive Christ as their Savior!

The next day at the medical clinics, the same mother came back with several of her friends and relatives to visit the clinics and receive prayer. She reminded me of the Samaritan woman in the Gospel of John who met Jesus at the well. Just like her, she ran off to tell everyone what Jesus had done. She told the governor's wife, the people at the kindergarten inauguration, all of her family and friends, and then they came to see what Jesus would do for them!

From Maine to Mexico

*And how shall they preach, except they be sent? as it is writ-
ten, How beautiful are the feet of them that preach the gospel of
peace, and bring glad tidings of good things!*
— *Romans 10:15 KJV*

On the last day of our mission trip, the Lord had a conversation
with me during prayer and worship time before going out to do
the medical mission. The Lord asked me, "Mike, who am I to
you?"

I replied, "Lord, You are my everything!"

Then He asked, "What will you do for me?"

I said, "Anything! Climb the highest mountain, swim the wid-
est sea!"

Then the Lord said, "I want you to come and live in Mexico and
pastor my sheep. I have many people who will come down for a
week or two, but very few will stay for the long haul."

I responded, "Whoa, that is a lot to ask. Lord, I am the assistant
pastor at the church You sent us to Maine to start up seven years
ago. Kim and I have been faithful, working hard to raise up the
church, and it's doing so well. Besides, we have two small children."

The Lord said, "But Mike, you said you would do anything for
Me."

Now, I'm really sweating and pondering the situation and
searching my soul. Finally, I replied, "Okay, I will say yes for myself, but You will need to talk to Kim. Since we are married and
have children, she must also agree to go."

I opened my eyes and decided to look at Kim, who was standing next to me, and I saw there were tears streaming down her
cheeks. I exclaimed to the Lord, "Lord, You are talking to her at
the same time You are talking to me!"

Later that day, I pulled Kim aside to tell her about my conversation with the Lord. She said, "I knew before we left on this trip
that the Lord had called us to Mexico as missionaries. But I told
the Lord, 'You are going to have to talk to Mike about this, not

me.'" And that He did!

It took us one year to pull enough support together to head off as missionaries to Mexico. We held an estate sale in the middle of a snowstorm in January and sold everything we owned except what we were taking with us and a few items we left behind with friends. We could only take what we could pack in suitcases to fly down.

In December of 1989, we loaded 12 suitcases on the airplane and flew down to the Acapulco airport. We landed and were waiting for the American missionary who was scheduled to pick us up. Two hours later, he still wasn't there, so we piled everything into a taxi and headed off to Puerto Marques, which is located just on the other side of the mountains from the city of Acapulco. All we had was the name of the American missionary and directions to one of the churches there.

The taxi dropped us off at the church, and as we looked around, there was no one to be found. So we just sat there hoping the pastor or a member of the church would come by. Soon a young man came by and informed us that the pastor was out but would be back soon.

I asked him about the American missionary and if he could take me to his house. He agreed to, so I walked with this young man, leaving Kim with our children sitting on their suitcases at the church. I found out later that leaving my wife and kids all by themselves on our first day in a new country didn't make her feel very safe, especially as she watched me walk off and disappear.

So I walked with the young man about ¾ of a mile just to find out that we had a little over five more miles to go! I pulled out some pesos and suggested we ride the bus. He flagged the next bus that was coming by, and we both hopped aboard.

We finally arrived at the American missionary's house just to find out that he wasn't home. So we left a note and returned to the church. We were relieved to see the American missionary standing and talking with Kim and the kids when we arrived. We loaded up a few suitcases to take with us and left the rest of our luggage at the church to pick up once we found a place for us to stay as a family.

When we arrived at the missionary's house, we found out it was a two-bedroom house. He had three children and we had two, so each family got to have one bedroom apiece. We got settled into our little bedroom, which was filled wall-to-wall with just our suitcases and the bed.

It was the month of December, and in Mexico, they celebrate the Virgin of Guadalupe for the first two weeks in December with loud music, firecrackers, and food. I can still remember that as I laid down to sleep that night after a very long day, I could hear all of the festival noise going on in the streets. I looked out the window and saw children running everywhere, laughing and screaming. Firecrackers were exploding, loud music was blaring, and it was almost midnight. I said to myself, "God, is this where You called us?" Day number one of our missionary adventure was now in the books!

Living Water

Jesus answered and said to her, 'If you knew the gift of God, and who it is who says to you, "Give Me a drink," you would have asked Him, and He would have given you living water.'
— John 4:10

When we first arrived in Mexico, we spoke very little Spanish, so we attended language school. The first thing our instructor, Luz Maria, said was, "From now on, we will only speak Spanish."

She then handed a newspaper to Kim and said, "Read me something!" At which point, Kim looked at Luz Maria and burst into tears. Our first month in Mexico adjusting to the culture with two small children had been a little stressful, to say the least.

Now Luz Maria looked at me and said, "Alright, you talk to me."

Speaking in broken Spanish, I said, "My name is Mike."

Luz Maria responded and said, "My name is Luz Maria, tell me more."

Then I said, "Umm, I am an American,"

Luz Maria replied, "I am Mexican, tell me more."

"I am a Christian."

She replied, "I am a Catholic. What is the difference between a Catholic and a Christian?"

"Umm, I have Jesus in my heart," I said.

"Very interesting, tell me more."

Then I replied, "I have Living Water."

Startled, Luz Maria said, "You have what?"

I said, "I have Living Water." As I looked at Luz Maria, I could see her eyes were quickly filling with tears. She picked up the newspaper and began to fan her face but then dropped the newspaper and ran out of the room!

I looked at Kim and asked, "What just happened?" Kim just shook her head. Five minutes went by before Luz Maria came back into the room. She had wiped off the mascara that was on her eyes and asked in English, "What is this Living Water? I want some."

We explained to her the Gospel message and how God had called us to be missionaries to Mexico. We quickly became friends, and after our first month of Spanish lessons was completed, she invited us to her house to continue teaching us Spanish and we taught her more about Jesus and the Word of Life.

Her marriage was in the throes of divorce. She explained how her husband worked in Mexico City, and the men he worked with would drink and then go to brothels for entertainment. She was so unhappy with him and the life he was living; however, he noticed a big change in her after meeting us.

He wanted to meet with us, so we gladly met with them both and shared the Gospel message with him as well. We also taught them new principles from Scripture to apply in their marriage, and their marriage was restored. Yet another miracle!

Our First Church Plant and the Demoniac

Suddenly, a man in the synagogue who was possessed by an evil
spirit cried out, 'Why are you interfering with us, Jesus of Naza-
reth? Have you come to destroy us? I know who you are—the Holy
One of God!' But Jesus reprimanded him. 'Be quiet! Come out of
the man,' he ordered. At that, the evil spirit screamed, threw the
man into a convulsion, and then came out of him.
— *Mark 1:23-25 NLT*

Our first church plant was in the village of Tres Palos, or Three
Trees in English. A small, poor village with dirt streets and no
running water except for a public water hydrant at the entrance
to the village. This made it interesting each night as we were leaving the village after our church service with two small children
in the car because the men would congregate at dusk around the
water hydrant. They would strip down to their underwear, soap
up, and bathe in the open air.

We started the church plant with a group of college students
who were on a mission trip with us while getting their doctorate
in missions. We rented a house to start the church plant, and the
group split up and went around house to house during the day
to visit with the people, share the Gospel, and pray for the sick.

One of the houses they visited had a daughter with a fever, and
she couldn't eat anything. They prayed for her, and by evening,
the fever left, she felt better, and was eating. At another house,
a little girl had worms from drinking contaminated water and
had a swollen stomach. They prayed for her, and that night, she
passed all the worms. The next day, she was visibly healed!

In the evenings, we would hold evangelistic services on the
front porch of the house, and the students would invite the people they visited during the day to attend. We heard testimony
after testimony of how God heard their prayers and healed them.
The college students shared their personal testimonies, stories
from the Bible, and we sang praises to the Lord.

After several nights of holding these open-air evangelistic services on the front porch of the house, many curious people would drift by to listen. Soon we heard testimonies of several alcoholics who had stopped drinking to come and hang out at the night meetings.

The following week, we decided it was time to hold a village-wide open-air meeting on the basketball court. We brought out music equipment and held a full-scale evangelistic service with about 30 minutes of music followed by more testimonies and the Gospel message. Many answered the invitation to receive Christ in their lives, and we invited them to attend the weekly church services at the house church.

At the close of the two-week mission trip, the students had to say goodbye and head back to the U.S. There was a lot of momentum and excitement during those two weeks as the students were busy evangelizing and making friends. Many lives were touched by the power of God. As a result, a new church was born!

This village had a lot of occult activity that was holding much of the village in spiritual darkness. In this part of Mexico, they had a belief in old ancient Shamon occult practices. There was a spiritualist church in the village that believed in the power of witchcraft, and they mixed it with religious customs. It was run by several ladies, and the village people would go there if they were sick or had an illness. They would perform a "cleansing" by taking a raw egg in the shell and rubbing it over their body from their head to their feet, and then breaking it open into a jar. Depending on what they saw, they would give a spiritual explanation of why you were ill and if you could be healed. By the way, they charged a lot of money for their services, and because the people were superstitious and desperate, they would seek them out for help.

Fast forward several years. We handed the church in Tres Palos over to Pastor Carlos to oversee. We ordained him at the young age of just nineteen years old! One day, when he was talking to the people in the village, they told him about a man named Boni who was forty years old and who lived down the street from where the spiritualist church was located. They told him that the man was crazy, was chained to a tree by his ankles, and that the spiritist church was not able to cure him.

Pastor Carlos took a few of our pastors with him to visit the family and see if they could help him. When they arrived, they were surprised to see his condition. The mother had him chained to a tree for the past 15 years, and he was unbathed and scantily dressed. The mother was very reluctant to allow them to talk to the man, much less pray for him. They decided they should come back later after spending some time in prayer.

Pastor Carlos decided to organize an all-night prayer meeting, inviting all five of the local churches and their pastors to gather for a night of worship and prayer. At around three o'clock in the morning, the pastors felt the leading of the Spirit to go and pray for Boni with the expectation that the Lord would set him free. So they set out to walk over to where Boni was chained to the tree. When they approached Boni that night, he was violent and aggressive and would throw things at them, holler at them, and spit at them. However, they were patient and persistent and stood their ground. They spoke the Word of God over him and prayed for him to be set free in the name of Jesus.

There didn't seem to be any immediate results, but they felt a determination from the Lord to persist in praying for Boni's deliverance. One hour passed, and then two hours passed, but they continued steadfastly, declaring the Word of God and the name of Jesus! In the third hour of prayer, they noticed a change in Boni's countenance. They were able to have a rational conversation with him and share God's love and explain God's will to set him free.

This time, when they prayed for him, God set him completely free! The mother could see that her son was no longer tormented and was in his right mind, so she took the chains off from his ankles! Before, he was violent and uncontrollable, but now he was calm, relaxed, and completely set free.

The following week, Pastor Carlos came back to visit the young man, and he was bathed, clothed, and had a smile on his face! Pastor Carlos invited Boni to attend his church so he could disciple him. It was amazing to see the transformation in this young man's life. For years he was left almost naked, filthy, and chained to a tree. He was violent and tormented, but now he was fully dressed, clean, and in his right mind.

We met Boni when we visited the church in Tres Palos on our quarterly missions trips and saw him take part in the church services by reading a scripture as they were taking up the offering. God is good, and He gave us a Name that is above all names—the name of Jesus—and He sets the captives free!

That at the name of Jesus every knee should bow, in heaven and on earth and under the earth, and every tongue declare that Jesus Christ is Lord, to the glory of God the Father.
— Philippians 2:10-11 NLT

Lord, Why Acapulco?

And He said to them, 'I saw Satan fall like lightning from heaven. Behold, I give you the authority to trample on serpents and scorpions, and over all the power of the enemy, and nothing shall by any means hurt you.'
— *Luke 10:18-19 NKJV*

When someone asks us where we are located as missionaries in Mexico, we are reluctant to say Acapulco because the first reaction we get is sarcasm: "Oh, that's got to be a tough assignment! You must have a beach ministry!" They really don't know how it truly is there.

Our ministry is located in the poorest villages in the area on the other side of the mountains from the city of Acapulco. Also, what most people aren't aware of is that Acapulco has been under the control of the cartels for several years. There have been times that we have arrived for a mission trip and were advised not to be on the streets that night because of cartel activity going on. As a result of all the violence, many of our church people were reluctant to go to church at night if the services didn't end before dark. So we had to change service times so they would come to church.

Acapulco used to have several branches of law enforcement. When the cartels swept into the city of Acapulco, their intimidation tactics caused most of the police force to side with the cartels and secretly work for them. In 2019, the Federal Government swept in and had all 1,100 men on the police force take a lie detector test, and 700 of them failed. They arrested all 700 of them and put them in jail. As a result, there are now only Federal police or Military soldiers. And what made it even more difficult was that it was nearly impossible to know who was in the police and who was in the cartel. Men dressed in police uniforms, held AK-47s, and had masks over their faces to protect their identity.

The police don't investigate crime down here like we are accustomed to in the USA. They are afraid of the cartels. Three of our church members lost their husbands to cartel violence and are now widows. All the police did when they were called to the scene was crowd control. They never looked for the shooters.

When we first arrived 34 years ago, Acapulco wasn't taken over by the cartels. We heard of a large Christian church in the city of Acapulco when we first moved down, and we went in to catch one of their church services. We quickly made friends with one of the families that attended the church, and they invited us to join them for Christmas Eve at their house.

They were so gracious. They even gave a present to each of our children. They asked us where we lived on the other side of the mountain and where our church was located. When we told them we had a church in Tres Palos, they were shocked because we were doing a work in a village that even the police wouldn't go to.

Tres Palos was a rough town. People were volatile, and it was uncertain how they would respond at different times. Once, we were doing an outreach on a basketball court with a group that came down to help us, and people threw rocks at us. A man was killed just down the street from our church one night. There were no police there, and there was no investigation into the incident.

It was stories like these that circulated and scared people away from bringing the Gospel message into Tres Palos, but we continued working in the village—a miracle in itself. God's miracle-working favor was upon us; the village people had accepted us—yet another miracle—and for all of this, we always felt safe.

Please Help Me Get My Baby Back!

...The Lord, in whose presence I have lived, will send his angel with you and will make your mission successful....
— Genesis 24:40 NLT

Life isn't always pretty or easy in the ministry, especially on the mission field. We had a situation where a woman approached us in a village where we have a church and asked for help. A few nights before this, her husband was drunk, they got into an altercation, he beat her badly, and left her unconscious in the street. After this, he took their newborn baby and ran off without a word of where he was going.

She asked us to take her to file a police report, and we gladly assisted her. Her face was so traumatized that she wouldn't go out in public without a towel over her head. A few days later, her husband snuck into the village and left a note with a neighbor that if she wanted to see her child, she would have to come to a village about two hours away that was only accessible by boat. She asked us if we could take her there and help her get her baby back.

We prayed about it and got the green light on the condition that we could bring two other people with us who knew this man and could help keep things calm. So we all piled into our jeep and off we went. We drove out to the dam where there were fishermen and hired them to take us in their canoe out to the island. It was about a 45-minute boat ride since they had to paddle us the entire way—no motor!

Once we reached the island, the woman knew where to find the house her husband was staying in. Before we arrived at the house, her husband suddenly rushed out from behind a tree and confronted us. He informed us that he had friends of his in strategic positions around the island, and they all had guns trained on us. He went on to tell us that if we tried anything, we would be shot. Needless to say, we assured him that we had no intentions of escalating the situation and we came in peace.

The mutual friends that came along were able to gain his confidence by speaking peacefully with him. They kept him subdued emotionally. Meanwhile, the mother of the child explained to him that for the baby to thrive, he needed breast milk. He finally agreed to allow the mother to be reunited with the baby and feed him.

We ended up spending several hours there with continued negotiations, and the father eventually agreed to let the baby go back with us and stay with its mother. Thank God! So our group headed back to find the fishermen and rehire them to take us back to the dam where our vehicle was parked. It was such a relief on the way back to see the mother joyfully reunited with her baby.

One of the fishermen asked us to wait for him while he was securing his canoe so we could give him a ride back to his house, which was on the way back to the main road. He seemed to be taking a long time, and we began to get an uneasy feeling. He finally showed back up, but he was carrying a .22-caliber rifle. He had the rifle with him in the boat, so it did make sense that he wanted to take it back with him to his house. However, something felt off about the situation, the way he was acting.

On the ride back, he seemed nervous, like he was contemplating something but wasn't sure of himself. So what did we do? We prayed in the Spirit and took authority over the situation. We arrived at his drop-off point, he slowly got out of the vehicle, and then simply walked away.

Thank You, Lord, for watching over us and giving us the victory in both situations!

I Can See!

The blind see and the lame walk; the lepers are cleansed and the deaf hear; the dead are raised up and the poor have the gospel preached to them.
— Matthew 11:5 NKJV

Yeya always had a smile on her face. Her circumstances didn't determine her happiness. Her happiness came from Jesus, her Savior and Lord. Yeya only stood about four feet and a few inches tall. She didn't have much money and lived about five miles away from the church. And yet, at 80-plus years of age, she didn't let that stop her.

Many times, she would hail a taxi for a ride. Though she had no money, she would let them know her age, that she had trouble walking, which prevented her from working, she had no husband—other than Jesus—and that she needed to get to church. Almost without fail, they would graciously give Yeya a ride. During her commute, she would become an evangelist, letting everyone in the taxi know that she loved her Lord. She shared stories of how good He had been to her. She'd offer to lead them to the Lord, and no matter their answer, she'd pray for them anyway.

In one particular mid-week service, she came to us asking for prayer. She was having trouble seeing anything without a blur. She told us that she had gone to the eye doctor and that he had told her that her eyes were dead and that he was surprised she could even see!

Well, Yeya wasn't having any of that! She was determined to see clearly so she could continue leading people to her Lord. She asked for prayer, and we agreed with her in faith.

The next Sunday, as Kim was entering the church, she was struck in the shin by a cane! Yeya stood with a huge smile and with her cane in hand said, "Don't you walk by me without saying hello! I can see you clearly!" The joy of the Lord was all over her.

She went on to explain that after we prayed for her, she went back to the doctor the very next day to check her eyes. The doctor wasn't happy to see her again so soon, as he had just told her there was nothing he could do for her. He reexamined her eyes and was shocked by the impossible.

Yeya went on to tell him the color of his shirt, even his eyes! "Could a blind person see that?" she asked. She immediately shared with the doctor that Jesus had healed her eyes, and it didn't cost her anything but to ask Him and believe that He would do it.

Yeya lived to be almost 100 years of age before she stepped over to be with Jesus. The lives that this humble, yet exuberant little woman impacted were innumerable. We're sure she heard, "Well done, my good and faithful servant!"

He's not Drunk as You Suppose…Anymore!

And whatever things you ask in prayer, believing, you will receive.
— *Matthew 21:22 NKJV*

We had a new family come to one of our churches, and we asked them where they lived because we wanted to visit them during the week. They reluctantly gave us some vague directions, so we decided we would just go and find where they lived.

When Kim and I arrived, we saw the father, Chucho, standing between two of his sons, and they appeared to be holding him up. I walked over to say hello and shake his hand when suddenly he fell over backwards, and the two boys labored to walk him into the house. Chucho was an alcoholic and was stone drunk. The entire family was completely embarrassed. They apologized over and over again for his condition, and we told them we completely understood and thought nothing less of them. We told them that we would be praying for him to be set free.

A few months later, during an evening church service, Chucho came crawling into the church. He was so drunk he couldn't even walk but slowly crawled up toward the front of the church as I was preaching. I stopped in the middle of my message and walked over to him and helped him stand up from the floor. He tried to say something, but he wasn't able to do much more than mutter a few words. I assured him that we loved him and had been praying for him. I laid hands on him right then and there and prayed for him to be set free from alcohol. Afterward, his family helped him out of the church service and on to his house.

Sometime later, there was a large men's event in Acapulco, and Chucho attended the event with me and several of the men from church, including two of his sons. That day, Chucho gave his heart to Jesus and was miraculously set free.

One day, when Chucho was working, cutting branches off a tree, he fell out of the tree and hit his head on a rock pile. When the people in the village saw him crawling on the ground, they just assumed that he'd returned to his old lifestyle. They didn't offer him any help, and he crawled into a building and was discovered sometime later.

He suffered a concussion along with bleeding on the brain. He was quickly admitted to a hospital for treatment, but they only monitored him and didn't operate to relieve the pressure on his brain from the bleeding.

We had just arrived in Mexico on one of our mission trips. At this time, it was much later in our ministry, and we were living back in the U.S., making quarterly trips to our churches. Upon our arrival, we got this news and went directly to the hospital to see him. In Mexico, only one person can go in and visit a patient at a time, and they only let you in for five minutes. His wife wanted me to go in and pray for him. I went in and found Chucho unconscious, so I laid hands on him and prayed for his recovery and left.

A few days went by, and we were having our Sunday morning church service when word came that the family should get his papers together because he was not expected to live much longer that day. However, Kim received a word from the Lord that morning in her prayer time before church saying that Chucho would live and not die and declare the glory of the Lord! So when she heard that report, she and I gathered everyone together. I told them what the Lord had said, and we all prayed in agreement for his recovery.

We left immediately after service to head to the hospital. Chucho's wife, Zenaida, asked me to go in and pray for him again. So I went in, and this time he was conscious. The nurse was talking to him and asked him what his name was. All he could manage was, "My name is... My name is...," and nothing more.

The nurse saw me come in and said, "Chucho, you have a visitor." I walked over and greeted him, "Hello, Chucho!" To the nurse's amazement, he responded and said, "Apostle Mike!" Before I entered, Chucho was laying there with his eyes closed, but when he heard my voice, the lights turned on in his head, his eyes opened up, and he began to speak clearly.

The nurse just stood there completely in wonderment, as we

carried on a conversation for several minutes. She eventually walked away, but came back with food and asked me if I'd feed him since, "I was doing such a good job." I agreed. The five-minute visitation time was extended to over an hour. I fed him his lunch and prayed for him again.

After I prayed for him, Chucho demanded that I give him my hand. So I held out my hand, and he reached over and grasped it and said, "I have to pray for you before you can go." So Chucho prayed for me, and then I left to go take the good news to his family.

They were all in the corridor wondering what was taking me so long to return. I spoke these three words to them: "All is well!" They had all been in prayer out in the corridor, and God heard their prayers! They all broke out with voices of spontaneous thanksgiving and praise to God.

In just a few days, Chucho was out of intensive care and into a regular hospital room, and even though he was hooked up to an IV, he walked around room to room, witnessing to the other patients about how God had healed him and set him free from a life of alcohol addiction—a walking miracle!

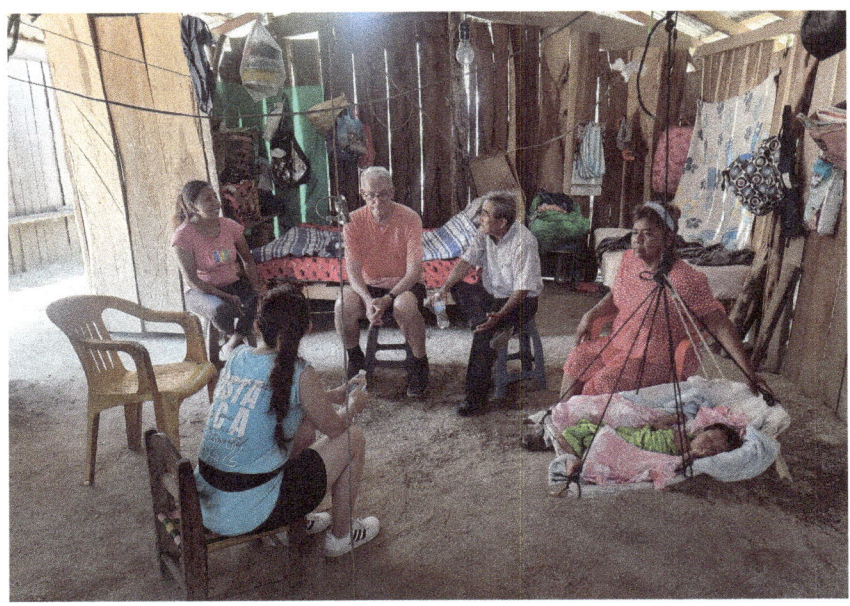

Stop! I Want You To Pray for Me!

The earnest (heartfelt, continued) prayer of a righteous man makes tremendous power available [dynamic in its working].
— *James 5:16^b AMPC*

Pastor Santiago, who Pastors two of our church plants, one in Puerto Marquez and the other in El Tamarindo, was traveling with his family to a wedding one afternoon and was passing through a mountainous village. As he drove by a particular house, the Lord told him to stop and pray for the man sitting in the front yard. Santiago said, "Lord, we are going to a wedding, and we are late! I can't stop now." The Lord said to him again, "Stop and pray for this man." So Santiago made a u-turn, introduced himself to the man, prayed for him, and then was off to the wedding.

The next day, they were passing back through the same village when a woman started running after them, hollering to stop. Santiago pulled over and asked her what she needed. She asked him if he was the pastor who drove through yesterday and prayed for this particular man. Santiago said yes.

She then explained that the man had a serious heart condition, and after Santiago prayed for him, he was completely healed! Naturally, she wanted Santiago to pray for her. He relayed that he'd love to, so he prayed for her, and went on his way.

The Lord laid it on their hearts to stop over and share the Gospel more completely with the people he had prayed for and their families. They were hungry for the Gospel message and invited him to come back whenever he could. During one of those visits, the people in the village asked him to consider buying a piece of land and building a church there. After praying about it, our ministry purchased a property that had a small house on it and space to build a church.

Over the next few years, he hired masons to build the new church. The church property is on the side of a hill, so they had to build a tall retention wall to serve as a foundation. Next they built the perimeter walls. Once that was completed, we put together a crew of ten men, and we spent a week out in El Tamarindo pouring the concrete floor and installing the metal roof. Today it is completely outfitted with all the necessities, including musical instruments!

Every Sunday morning, Santiago and his family would get up at 5:00 a.m., hop in their Volkswagen Beetle, and drive four hours to get to El Tamarindo by 9:00 a.m. They'd hold a church service at 10:00 a.m., followed by a meal with the members of the church. At that point they'd spend time discipling them for a few hours, and then make the four-hour trip back home.

Mexico has a rainy season and a dry season. The dry season is from November to May, and it generally doesn't rain a drop. Then from June through October is the rainy season. The last one-hour stretch of the road into El Tamarindo is a dirt road with very steep inclines along with some low-lying areas.

During the rainy season, it makes travel into the village very challenging. There were several times Santiago and his family couldn't drive their Volkswagen Beetle all the way to El Tamarindo because the road was too muddy or was flooded with water. So they left their car parked as far as they could drive it and walked the rest of the way, wading through the water or trekking through the mud. No, the life of a missionary isn't always glamorous. These pastors have hearts filled with the love of Jesus, and just like Him, they are filled with compassion to bring the light of the Gospel to the world. We Love you, brothers and sisters in El Tamarindo!

The Woman Who Couldn't Swallow

*And these signs will follow those who believe: In My name
they will cast out demons; they will speak with new tongues;
they will take up serpents; and if they drink anything deadly, it
will by no means hurt them; they will lay hands on the sick, and
they will recover.*
— *Mark 16:17-18 NKJV*

Pastor Carlos is our youngest pastor, and besides pastoring the church in Tres Palos, he has been the director of our Bible School, Escuela Bíblica Revelación, or Bible School Revelation, for the past fifteen years! He has a sign on the front of the church that advertises prayer for healing.

A woman, Beatriz, was riding by the church on a bus and saw the sign. She quickly ran to the front of the bus and had the driver stop to let her off. She had something wrong with her throat and wasn't able to swallow, so she was slowly starving to death.

She knocked on the door of the church and asked to speak with the pastor. Carlos and his wife, Irene, invited her in. After she explained what was happening, Pastor Carlos and Irene shared the Gospel with her and explained that it was "the double cure." She could receive salvation and healing at the same time! Jesus took both her sins and infirmities when He died on the cross. There's no need to continue bearing either since He bore both!

She prayed the salvation prayer with them, and they laid hands on her and prayed for healing. She was instantly healed! She went home that night and was able to eat just like she could before!

Needless to say, Beatriz came back to church with her family and continues to be a strong member of Carlos's church. Her daughter, Kenya, has been to the Bible school and was their youth pastor for several years. We see Beatriz every time we visit the church in Tres Palos, and she is yet another one of God's signs and wonders!

Natalia's Miracle

I shall not die, but live, and declare the works of the Lord.
— Psalm 118:17

Pastor Carlos has a brother named Tello. Tello is married to Mary, and together they have a miracle daughter by the name of Natalia. Natalia was born with several life-threatening diseases. Due to the number of diseases she had, it became difficult for physicians to even detect which types of diseases she had completely.

One of the many diseases she had was encephalitis, which caused her head to swell abnormally. This led to embarrassment for Tello and Mary because of the looks, questions, and hurtful comments they received every time they left home with Natalia. They eventually began putting a hat on her to try and hide the effects of the disease. Eventually, it wore them down to the point of not even wanting to take her to church.

Another effect of the many life-threatening diseases she was born with was that she was becoming more and more crippled. At twenty months of age, she wasn't crawling, rolling over, or sitting up. She was very weak physically and appeared anemic and undernourished. She could barely even digest food properly, much less hold it down.

Her condition continued to get worse, so they took her to see a specialist and found that on top of all the diseases, she also had a heart problem and a blood disease. His prognosis didn't paint a good future for Natalia, and when we found out about all of this on one of our trips, we made it a point to see her and pray for her.

When we arrived, they had her in a bed, lying on her back. Tello and Mary told us everything the doctors had said. After they finished, Kim told them everything that Jesus had to say!

Kim relayed that Natalia could absolutely live a healthy life, contrary to what the doctors said. She wasn't born to be crippled or disease-ridden! She went on to say that Jesus already paid the price, already bore every disease, and already healed her. Faith requires action! We came to pray, but it would be their job to continue in faith after we were gone.

We laid hands on and prayed over Natalia, and then Kim explained how keeping the faith included speaking what God says, the Word of God, over her and encouraging her to do what she couldn't do! She can't just lay there, and as her parents, they couldn't just allow her to. Kim then demonstrated right then and there by speaking directly to Natalia. She spoke to her and spoke over her that she would begin to roll over, sit up, and crawl. As she said these different actions, she would roll Natalia over, put her hands by her feet and gently nudge her legs, and rock her back up toward a sitting position.

We were there with them for a few hours, encouraging them with the Word of God. They had faith, but they needed to see how to use their faith and put it into action. Kim reinforced that they needed to speak over Natalia what she should be able to do, put their hands on her, and show her how to do it. Then all they had to do was watch God do what He does best—perform miracles!

Our trips are usually only for two weeks at a time, and then we leave to return to the U.S. So before we left, we gave her parents and her grandma, Eugenia, an assignment, a faith assignment. Grandma had already been healed of cancer a few years earlier and she had faith in her heart. She was completely on board for God to heal her granddaughter.

So when we returned three months later, we stopped in to see how Natalia was doing. She was thriving! She was able to roll over and had started basic moves toward crawling, getting stronger and stronger by the day.

We spent a few hours with them, encouraging them in the Word of God, giving them scriptures to stand on and speak over Natalia. Kim worked with her and spoke over her as she had done just three months before. We could feel the faith and excitement. Everyone was completely confident that Natalia would be completely healed in no time!

We will never forget what we saw when we walked into the church of Tres Palos the next time we visited. There was Natalia, sitting up on the tile floor in the middle of the church with a big smile on her face. When she saw us, she scooted towards us still in a sitting position! Her parents were beaming.

Just before we left to go back to the States, we told her parents that the next time we see them, Natalia will be walking—and that is exactly what happened! On our next trip down, when we walked into the church at Tres Palos, Natalia came running over to us and gave us big hugs!

Today, Natalia is 12 years old. She goes to school just like every other child, and she is completely normal. Every time we visit, she runs to us and gives us big hugs.

Raised From the Dead!

But taking her by the hand he called, saying, "Child, arise."
And her spirit returned, and she got up at once. And he directed
that something should be given her to eat. And her parents were
amazed, but he charged them to tell no one what had happened.
— Luke 8:54-56 ESV

Pastor Nolberto's daughter's wedding was quickly approaching, so he and his family were making last-minute preparations for the grand event. Every father wants to make sure his daughter's wedding will be an event to remember, and every daughter wants everything to be just wonderful as well. Pastor Nolberto is the Pastor of the church in Colonial del PRI, and he has been with our ministry since 1991.

It was the day before the wedding, and Pastor Nolberto wanted to do some last-minute painting in his house to make everything look just right. He was using a makeshift, home-built ladder to paint the high places on the stairway that leads up to the second floor. His son had just been up the ladder but didn't feel comfortable reaching the highest places, so Pastor Nolberto volunteered to take over.

As he was stretching to reach the last few places remaining, the ladder snapped, and he came tumbling down the ladder backwards. He landed upside down, directly hitting his head and shoulders on the concrete steps. His wife, Aida, had been holding the ladder steady for him, and she screamed as she lunged to grab him as he tumbled down the ladder but was unable to soften the blow.

She asked repeatedly if he was alright, but he wasn't able to say a word, only mumble a few noises. The rest of the family was nearby, and they all came running to his aid. They picked him up and carried him to the couch and began to pray for him.

That's when his eyes rolled back, and he went into convulsions. They grabbed a towel and tried to keep his mouth open so he wouldn't swallow his tongue, but they were unsuccessful. His body went limp, and he sank back into the couch. The family was frantic, not knowing what to do next.

They grabbed a bottle of rubbing alcohol and poured some on the towel. They placed it up to his nose to get him to respond, but all the efforts seemed hopeless. He had stopped breathing, and he lay there not moving a muscle. They began to shake him and call out to him, "Nolberto! Nolberto! Wake up! Wake up!" But there was no response. They all began to pray as they were also crying, "Lord, bring Nolberto back to us!"

Nolberto had left his body. He was now in Heaven and found himself talking to other family members who had gone on before him. He was surrounded by the beauty of Heaven, and as he was taking it all in, he heard them say, "What are you doing here? You can't stay; your family needs you."

The next thing he knew, he could see his family gathered around him praying for him, and he realized he was back in his house, looking down from above. They were earnestly praying for him, and suddenly he took a deep breath and opened his eyes. His family broke out in thanksgiving.

Now that he was stabilized, they loaded him into a car and took him to the hospital, where he was examined by the medical staff and treated for his injuries. He stayed there several days recuperating from the fall. Besides his concussion, he had torn muscles in his shoulder, but he made a complete recovery!

Healed of Stage 4 Cancer

The thief cometh not, but for to steal, and to kill, and to destroy: I am come that they might have life, and that they might have it more abundantly.
— John 10:10 KJV

Eugenia is one of our precious church members who deserves so much credit for what she has overcome in life. She grew up in a remote mountain village 6 hours north of our ministry. She was in the final days of her pregnancy with her fourth child when her husband was shot dead on the doorstep of her house in her village. Four hours later she gave birth to Pastor Carlos. She left Carlos in the care of her mother and fled from the village to start a new life with her three other children on the other side of the mountains from Acapulco. A few years later, she sent for Carlos to be reunited with the rest of his family.

She squatted on a piece of land, basically a swamp, and started hailing dump trucks giving them permission to dump their loads of backfill on her property for free. She spent her days spreading the loads of backfill, and with the help of others, eventually built a house for herself and her children. Several years later she came to know the Lord through our ministry and has been a strong church member ever since.

She is a mother of four, a grandmother of ten, and a great-grandmother of three. This is the same grandmother from "Natalia's Miracle Story," and she had great faith for the healing of her granddaughter as well. She lives a simple life but feels like she owns the world and loves to serve the Lord in any way she can. She loves evangelizing and telling people how much God loves them, and she uses her testimony every step of the way.

It was a warm and sunny day as we landed in Mexico on one of our trips to minister to the people and check on the pastors and the churches. As part of our routine, we headed to the house of Eugenia, where we stored our coolers and a few things we used each trip when we were in Mexico. So, naturally, her house was usually one of the first stops.

On this particular trip she was excited, more than usual, to see us. She asked (me) Kim to come sit with her because she had something she wanted to share with me. So I sat with her as she proceeded to tell me that she'd been asking God for a testimony. She was so excited to say He had given her one.

She began to tell me that God had given her uterine cancer but not to worry because He was going to heal her and that would be her testimony. I gently put my finger to her lips and asked her to be still. I proceeded to tell her that God couldn't give her cancer—that would be impossible. God cannot give you what he doesn't have. I told her that God is a good God and He only gives good things to His children. I quoted John 10:10 to her: "The thief cometh not, but for to steal, and to kill, and to destroy: I am come that they might have life, and that they might have it more abundantly." The devil is the thief and he is trying to kill you, a faithful servant of God.

As we sat and talked, I gave her scriptures to read daily. I also gave her confessions to say like, "I am the healed of the Lord" and, "no weapon formed against me will prosper" and, "since God is my healer, I am healed" and, "I will have a great testimony of the healing power of God."

On our next trip, I brought down books and CDs in Spanish with the assignment that she was to listen to and read and confess the Word of God over herself daily and all throughout the day. I also told her to keep the CDs playing 24 hours a day so she'd be feeding her spirit even while sleeping. Eugenia was full of faith and took her assignments very literally. Every spare moment she filled herself to overflowing with the word of God and made declarations of the healing power of her Lord and Savior.

When she went to the doctor, they decided to not operate on her but to treat her with chemotherapy. She was happy to not have an operation and told the doctors that she would have no side effects from the chemo. She boldly claimed that she would not feel sick and would not even lose a hair off her head. As treatments proceeded, she got exactly what she was saying. There were no ill side effects and she kept all her hair.

The Doctor's were amazed and said she was one strong woman.

Her response was, "I have a very strong and faithful God!" At the completion of treatments, the doctors told her she was cancer free and that they had never met anyone with faith like hers. She still reads one of the books that I gave her. She looks at it as still taking and using the Word so no future attack will get her. She's staying loaded with the Word of God!

The Man Who Couldn't Talk

And if we know that He hears us, whatever we ask, we know
that we have the petitions that we have asked of Him.
— 1 John 5:15 NKJV

One day, Chucho—yes, the same Chucho who was healed from a brain injury—was walking by our churches in Llano Largo and noticed a man sitting in a chair in front of his house right next to the church. The man motioned for Chucho to come to him as he was passing by.

Jaime, the man who was seated, had suffered a stroke, was paralyzed on his left side, and could no longer talk. Chucho understood that Jaime had suffered a stroke by the noises and motions he was using to attempt to communicate. He was trying to express that he wanted Chucho to pray for him.

Jaime lived in the house right next to the church, but he never attended a single service. As a matter of fact, he would mock anyone who went to church. Jaime finally came to terms and realized he needed a touch from God.

Chucho laid his hands on him, prayed for him, and then went on his way. The next day, as Chucho walked by, Jaime motioned for him to stop and pray for him again. So he did. The day after that, Chucho was walking by, and Jaime was able to speak a few words!

Chucho took this opportunity and shared the Gospel message with Jaime, along with his testimony of how God had miraculously healed him. Jaime accepted Christ right then and there. A few days later, he was completely healed! There was no sign that he had ever suffered a stroke!

The next time we were at the church in Llano Largo, Jaime greeted us and shared how gracious God had been to him and how he was made whole from the stroke. God's goodness on display once again!

PERSONAL MIRACLES AND TESTIMONIES

This next section is a collection of personal testimonies, stories, and miracles that
have happened to our family and some of those of the pastors under our ministry. You'll find that some of them happened on the mission field, and some are personal stories that put the amazing, miraculous power of God on display.

MIKE DAVIS

The Day I Saw Heaven

Giving thanks unto the Father, which hath made us meet to be partakers of the inheritance of the saints in light: Who hath delivered us from the power of darkness, and hath translated us into the kingdom of his dear Son.
— Colossians 1:12-13 KJV

I was a bit of a wild child in my youth. I loved adventure and wanted to experience life in its fullness. I was in the thick of the Jesus Revolution, in the late '60s and early '70s. My hair was long and I wore bell bottoms. And true to form, during this time, I had begun to experiment with drugs.

As time went on, I began to get more involved with hard drugs, such as LSD and synthetics. I knew that if I continued down that path, I couldn't expect to live for much longer. So I decided to quit. I quit drugs, alcohol, and cigarettes. I wanted to see what life was like without them.

At the time, I was working in a textile factory, and every day for lunch I would ride my ten-speed bike out to a place I had found in a field. I'd bring my sack lunch and radio and just listen to music or Paul Harvey's the Rest of the Story.

One afternoon, I was crossing the same field, as I had grown accustomed to doing, and, suddenly, I felt joy bubble up inside me. I had no idea what was happening. I was no stranger to a feeling of euphoria, having used drugs, but it had been over a week since the last time I had used anything.

I looked to Heaven and said, "Thank you, God, for today." When I said that, the sky opened up before my eyes and I saw what looked like a magnificent city. There was a stream of glory that emanated from this beautiful city that captured my heart. God didn't speak a single word, but more than words could ever say, He showed me how glorious and majestic the Kingdom of God is in the vision I was seeing.

I cried out, "God! There is nothing on earth that compares to

41

what you just showed me. This is what I've been looking for all of my life! I want to be with You! Take me up to You!"

Having seen enough Star Trek, I was expecting God to "beam me up," but that's not what happened. Instead, I felt an explosion go off inside me, and I didn't beam upward at all. No, I fell. I fell completely off of my bike and onto the ground. My heart was racing and all I could do was question what had just happened!

I eventually got up off the ground, got back up onto my bike, and went on to the spot where I always sat and had lunch. I listened to the radio and Paul Harvey and then went back to work—business as usual. But not really!

I was transformed that day by the grace and glory of God. I never wanted drugs again! All I wanted was another touch from Heaven! I would find myself talking to God throughout the day. I would stop to pray and just ask for another glimpse of that beautiful city. I wanted to experience more of what God had. I needed it.

I grew up in the Catholic church, and they talked about God, but no one ever said that they knew God or had met God. My first thought after experiencing all I had experienced was that I needed to find some people who really knew God! I knew I needed to be around those types of people.

Summer was ending and college was about to start. I had determined within myself that I was going to make friends with people who knew God. I wasn't looking to return to the old crowd of drugs, alcohol, cigarettes, and swearing. I bought a cross to wear around my neck and I drew crosses on my textbooks. I was looking for anyone who knew God and hoping all of my crosses would draw their attention!

One day at lunch, I struck up a conversation with a guy who I learned to be a Christian. He told me about a Christian Fellowship that he was a part of, called InterVarsity. He asked if I'd be interested in going with him and that he'd pick me up and take me. I eagerly agreed.

We went to a prayer meeting before the fellowship meeting. I learned, as I watched everyone else pray, that praying was easy. It was just having a conversation! So I jumped right in and began to talk to God in prayer! "This is awesome," I thought. And just like that day in the field, I began to feel that same joy bubble up on the inside of me once again.

I decided that I should start attending church, and since I was Catholic, that I should go to a Catholic church. However, Catholics also go to confession the Saturday night before church to be absolved of their sins. So off I went to the church to say my confession. When I went into the confessional booth to confess my sins, to my amazement, I couldn't think of anything I had done wrong. I couldn't think of anything to tell the priest!

So, instead of confessing, I sat inside the confessional and fumbled through an explanation of my hunger to want to know God more, my vision of Heaven, the bubbly joy, that I had found some friends, and that I had learned to pray. After all that, I still couldn't think of anything to confess.

The priest told me to come to church tomorrow, but after that, to find a church near campus and I would find more friends my age. So I did. I attended church that Sunday morning and the priest taught a message called The Five Things God Wants Us To Do. Among those five things was to read our Bible. I didn't even have a Bible!

As I was riding my bike back to campus, I was pondering the idea of reading the Bible. A few weeks before, I had caught the end of a Billy Graham program where they offered a free Bible. All I had to do was write in and ask. In that moment, I remembered that I did write in and ask! So I prayed, God, if you want me to read the Bible, I want to find a Bible in my mailbox tomorrow when the mail comes.

In great anticipation, the next day, I went to the mailbox and opened it to find the Bible I had requested! That settled it. It was time to start reading and studying my Bible. There were several study lessons in the back of the Bible with references that helped me on my journey to know God more and more each day.

The Glory of God Filled the Room

Now the Lord is that Spirit: and where the Spirit of the Lord is, there is liberty. But we all, with open face beholding as in a glass the glory of the Lord, are changed into the same image from glory to glory, even as by the Spirit of the Lord.
— 2 Corinthians 3:17-18 KJV

My conversion experience happened in the summer of 1974. During Christmas break of the same year, I was spending time with a friend one evening. We were worshiping the Lord together, singing songs and such, when suddenly there was a bright light that appeared in the corner of the room.

The glory of God filled the room with His majesty and holiness. It was just like the glory I saw coming from the city the day I saw Heaven! At first, we basked in the manifest presence of God's glory. I had to close my eyes because the brilliance of the light of the glory was so bright. Even with my eyes closed, the light penetrated through. It grew brighter and brighter. And just like when you get closer and closer to a campfire or fireplace on a chilly night, the flames of the bright burning fire are so warm and inviting. You just want to draw closer and closer and stare into the flickering flames.

The glory of God continued to grow stronger and stronger. I could feel it penetrating my heart and soul all the way down to the core of my innermost being. It was just like the refiner's fire that's mentioned in Malachi 3:2.

At first, this refiner's fire was so warm and inviting, but the intensity was building higher and higher. I found myself squeezing my eyes tighter and tighter, but it was to no avail. The glory of God continued to grow brighter and brighter.

When the glory first entered the room, I knew it was Him. There was such a warm embrace of His loving kindness, tenderness, and mercy. His love is perfect and all-consuming. It was a love that I had never known before.

My parents were strict and used old-fashioned tough love to try and shape and mold me over the years. Of course they loved me, but I can never remember ever hearing the words, "Son, I love you," or, "I'm proud of you," or, "You make me happy." I also never remember being hugged or embraced by either of my parents growing up. It was a combination of the fact that I needed a lot of correction and that my parents didn't know how to express their affection openly.

As the glory of God continued to fill the room, I was absorbing all of this beautiful love, and it began to fill that empty void inside of me. It was a healing love that spoke loudly and was so affirming. However, as the intensity continued to grow stronger and stronger, I became less and less in control of myself. I suddenly fell to the floor and lay prostrate before Him.

His presence was so great and overwhelming that I felt it would consume me like fire consumes the wood in a campfire. I lay on the floor until the presence of the glory of God lifted. It was an experience that has marked my life forever. That day, I experienced the glory and majesty of God along with His infinite greatness, or at least as much as I could handle!

God Heals Broken Bones!

Therefore I say to you, whatever things you ask when you pray,
believe that you receive them, and you will have them.
— *Mark 11:24*

I worked as a carpenter early on in our marriage, and one day I was jacking up the second floor of a barn to replace a rotted sill when suddenly the jack slipped, and the concrete-filled steel post struck my wrist, pinning it up against the 2x4 framing of the wall. I felt a sharp pain in the interior of my wrist as I grabbed it and took a moment to collect myself. The pain seemed to dwindle away, and there was no immediate swelling, so I chalked it up to a close call.

However, the following week, we were working on another part of the barn, replacing another sill that was in bad shape. As a co-worker and I were lifting a heavy beam into position, suddenly I felt a sharp pain and weakness in my wrist. From that point on, I noticed there was some swelling, and as time went on, it was painful to even try to move my thumb in an open position. A few weeks later, when the swelling and pain persisted, I told my boss what was going on, so he made an appointment for me to see an orthopedic.

When the doctor took a close look at the X-ray, he turned to me and said, "How long have you had this broken wrist?" To my amazement, I replied, "What broken wrist?" The doctor said, "Your wrist has been broken for some time now. When a bone breaks, there are rough, uneven edges, and the edges on the navicular bone in your wrist are worn smooth." I explained to the doctor the series of events with the jack slipping and when I lifted the heavy beam and the pain and swelling. The doctor didn't have good news for me. He explained that this small bone in my wrist won't be an easy one to heal because of the small amount of blood flowing through that bone and how the two pieces of the broken bone had been rubbing together for some time now and no longer fit together like puzzle pieces.

The doctor said, "We will put a cast on for 6 weeks and see what happens." So he put a cast on my left wrist, and I went back to work. Six weeks later, they took the cast off and X-rayed my wrist, and there was no improvement. The doctor said the next step would be a bone graft, and they would need to take bone marrow from my hip and put it in my wrist along with a pin to hold it in place. They would then put a cast on my wrist again, but this time for three months, and I would have to be off from work and resting during that time.

So I had the bone graft operation, and a cast was put on my left wrist, and I was sent home to rest and not work. However, I'm not someone who can easily just sit around. Soon I started to make some end tables in the basement of the house, being careful not to use my left arm to lift with. However, one day the door to the closet came off track, so I decided to lift it back up into place using both arms. As I lifted up the door, I felt a sharp pain in my left wrist. As I winced, I thought to myself, Oh no! I hope I didn't just mess up the operation.

When three months were finally up, I went back to have the cast removed and my wrist X-rayed, and they discovered that my wrist hadn't healed and the bone was still broken. It was very painful to try and move my wrist, and I asked the doctor what he recommended that we do. The doctor explained that he could perform another bone graft, but the chances of success were only 40 percent now. I said, "Let me think about that and I'll get back with you."

I explained to Kim what the doctor had said, and we both agreed we needed to seek the Lord and see what He wanted us to do. I said to Kim, "There is no way I want to go through another operation and three more months with a cast."

A short time later, a friend invited me to attend a meeting where there was teaching on divine healing followed by prayer. I thought to myself, "I need to go!" So we went to the meeting, and I was amazed by the teaching of faith in God and the Word of God he was preaching. I had never heard someone teach with such faith and authority.

When the preacher said, "I'll never be sick another day in my life," the first thought that went through my mind was, "You liar!"

You can't say that! Everybody gets sick from time to time. Why, I get sick every February with a cold for about a week." It seemed that the more that preacher taught on healing, every doubt that I had about being healed was being confronted. At the end of the message, the preacher invited anyone who needed healing to come forward for prayer.

I went forward, and when the preacher asked me what I needed, I explained I had a broken wrist. The preacher asked me, "Do you believe that the moment I lay hands on you to be healed, God will heal you?" I thought about that for a moment, and my head responded saying no, but my spirit quickly spoke up and said yes! The word that came out of my mouth was yes. Then the preacher laid hands on me and said several times, "Just receive it, just receive it, just receive it."

At that moment, I had a conversation with God: "God, what does he mean just receive it? I don't understand." God replied, "What did he just teach you? That when you pray, believe that you receive, and you will have whatsoever you pray." I thought, I can do that. So I said, "Lord, I receive." When I said those words back to God, an explosion went off inside me: "I've got it! I'm healed!" Right at that moment, I didn't feel anything happen to my wrist, just an assurance in my heart that I was healed.

On the way back to the house, I was greeted by a neighbor, and she asked how my day was going. I responded, "Wonderful! God healed my wrist today!" "Really?" Then she asked, "How does it feel?" I replied, "Just like it did before, why?" "Oh," she replied, "It's one of those faith healings. I tried that once and it didn't work for me. I hope it does for you." Then she walked off. Her words didn't sit well at all with me. In fact, they got my dander up quite a bit.

As I walked into our apartment, I thought to myself, "What could a healed person do? He could do pushups." At that time, I couldn't bend my wrist all the way back; it was mostly in a straight position. So I thought, "I can do push-ups on my knuckles." So I got down on my fists and started doing push-ups: 1, 2, 3, 4, and each time my chest went down toward the floor, my wrist would make a clicking sound, but that didn't stop me until I did ten push-ups. When I finished, I stood up and said, "See, I'm healed in Jesus' name!"

A few days later, the same neighbor asked me for a favor. "Mike, I need to move a chair from my second floor apartment down to the main office. Can you help me carry it down?" Then she remembered our conversation from a few days ago about God healing my wrist. "Oh, I just remembered about your wrist. I don't want to test your faith." Whereupon I replied, "Don't be concerned; my wrist is doing just fine," and I helped carry the chair all the way to the main office. From that day on, my wrist was completely healed by faith in Jesus and the Word of God.

Healed by Faith in God's Amazing Love

*That Christ may dwell in your hearts through faith; that you,
being rooted and grounded in love, may be able to comprehend
with all the saints what is the width and length and depth and
height—to know the love of Christ which passes knowledge; that
you may be filled with all the fullness of God.*
— *Ephesians 3:17-19 NKJV*

When our daughter Andrea was finishing high school, we moved back to Bixby, Oklahoma, for her senior year. I worked as a self-employed remodeling contractor along with my son and called my company Davis & Son Remodeling. I landed a large roofing job for a two-story house, and the very first week of the job, I hurt my right knee. It hurt to walk, and I couldn't climb up or down the ladder. It was also the leg I used to push the gas pedal, and it hurt to even push the pedal to drive.

I was perplexed at the situation because there was no way that my son could strip and shingle this roof all by himself. We were tearing off wood shingles and installing new OSB sheathing and then installing 40-year architectural shingles. All I could do was limp around on the ground and cut the OSB sheathing and hand it up to him while he was doing most of the work.

Meanwhile, as I was standing around on the ground watching my son hard at work, I was considering my options. What am I going to do? This is only week two of this job, and we are only on side two of the roof and not even 25-percent done. I can't go see a doctor; he's going to tell me what type of injury I have and most likely will want me to have an operation, and that will set me back weeks or months.

I began to cry out in my heart, "God, I need you to heal my knee!" I was praying, praying, and praying throughout the entire day, day after day, all that week. I was calling on God to heal my knee as I limped around helping my son as much as I could.

Meanwhile, Kim left earlier that week and flew up to Maine to drive her father from Maine to Florida where he had his house. He was too old to drive himself all that distance by himself, so

Kim went to be his chauffeur. She then flew from Florida back to Oklahoma at the end of the week. So, on Friday, I headed to the airport to pick her up.

As I said, I had been praying nonstop for God to heal my knee; however, as I was driving to the airport, my knee was screaming in pain. The thought that ran through my head was, God, I know you love me, and because you love me, you can and will heal my knee. So I began saying at the top of my lungs while driving down highway 169 toward the airport, "God, I know you love me! I know you love me! I know you love me!" Then every time I screamed that out, I would slap my knee and say, "I am healed! God, I know you love me!" I slapped my knee and said, "I am healed!"

This went on for several minutes until I felt inside me that I had released my faith for my healing. When I got to the airport, I mistakenly parked at the wrong end of the terminal and had to walk to the other side of the airport to get to the terminal where Kim was waiting for me. I only got about halfway and was in so much pain I had to stop and wait about 5 minutes or so for the pain to diminish. I finally resumed walking and found Kim, and then we had to walk all the way back again, me limping, all along the way, slowly!

I explained to Kim what had happened, and we got caught up on her journey driving her dad to Florida on the ride home. It was late and time for bed, so we both climbed in bed and said goodnight. I tried to get comfortable but couldn't find a position where my knee didn't hurt so I could sleep.

I didn't want to keep Kim awake, so I got up and went out and laid on the couch. I said, "God, I know you love me; I know you love me," and I felt Him direct me to put my knee in a certain position, and when I did, the pain was gone, and I fell asleep. That seemed to help for a little while, but then the pain returned, and I sensed He said, "Move it this way," and when I did, the pain left and I fell back to sleep. This went on all night. I would sleep, move, sleep, move, sleep, and move.

When it was morning, I got up off the couch, and the pain in my knee was completely gone. It was like God was my chiropractor all night long, having me move from position to position, and by morning, I was healed!

The following Monday, I was off to work and climbed the ladder to the second floor with bundles of shingles on my shoulder, and I was pain-free and 100-percent healed. We finished the job on time, and one thing I know for sure: God loves me!

KIM DAVIS

My Best Friend, God

So then, since we have a great High Priest who has entered heaven, Jesus the Son of God, let us hold firmly to what we believe. This High Priest of ours understands our weaknesses, for he faced all of the same testings we do, yet he did not sin.
— *Hebrews 4:14-15*

I was born and raised Catholic in Maine. We were very Catholic. In fact, my aunt was a Nun. Needless to say, church wasn't an option growing up. Every Saturday evening, we would go to confession. We'd confess our sins to the Priest, and he would tell us our penance. Usually, it consisted of three to five Hail Mary prayers, a few Our Father prayers, and the Rosary. All of this combined qualified you to take communion on Sunday morning. So, week after week, this was our routine.

One Saturday evening when I was six years old, we were told to get ready to go to the church for confession. Now, I wasn't a bad kid. In fact, I didn't like being in trouble and tried hard to not get in trouble. On this particular Saturday evening, I ran upstairs to my bedroom and found myself saying, "Lord, I don't know what to do. I don't remember doing anything wrong this week. I try really hard to be good. In fact, I'm going to have to make up a lie to the priest and then confess that what I just told him was my real sin. What should I do?"

I'm still in my room, not realizing that I had started a conversation with the Lord. After I spurt out my thoughts, I heard in my spirit, "You don't need to confess your sins to the priest; just talk with me, and I will forgive you." I knew it was God talking to me, and I ran downstairs to tell my Mom the good news.

To my surprise, my mom slapped my face and told me that she would not have blasphemy spoken in the house. Then she asked me who I thought I was, thinking I could directly talk with God. It was too late. I knew that God had spoken to me, and I was forever marked. In fact, I began talking with God several times a day. He became my best friend. My childhood wasn't easy, and God became a close companion for me—a safe place to share my heart and feelings and know that He cared.

During my junior year of high school, I was working in the local nursing home as an aide. One evening, I worked the 3:00 p.m. to 11:00 p.m. shift, and a blizzard hit while I was working. At 11:00 p.m., when it was time to leave, two feet of snow had fallen! I lived two miles from work, but I wasn't about to stay any longer than I had to. The last time I worked all night, someone died, and there was no way I was going to deal with all that again!

The roads were undriveable, so I decided to walk. I rounded a corner on my way and noticed all the lights on at the Baptist Church. I also spotted my neighbor's car in the parking lot, so I went inside, hoping to catch a ride as soon as the roads cleared. As I entered the church, I noticed several people rocking in rocking chairs—undeniably a strange and unexpected sight to see at 11:00 p.m.

I approached my neighbor to ask what she was doing and to see if I could catch a ride when she left. I learned that she was going to be there all night because they were sponsored to "rock all night" in order to raise money for mission work in other nations.

Before all of this, my grandmother, my dad's mom, was always giving me books to read about people who lived in other nations and how they helped people. I was intrigued and always excited to read the next book. They touched me deeply, and I found myself talking to God about them and that someday I would like to impact people just like the people in those books. It didn't occur to me then that these people were missionaries.

By morning, I found myself talking to God as I had become accustomed to. I relayed to Him that if He could do something, anything, with my sister, then I would serve Him the rest of my life. At this point, my sister was mixed up in drugs and marijuana. One week after I prayed this prayer, my sister got saved! Such a very quick answer to prayer, to which my response was, "You got me, Lord! I'm all yours! I give you my life; now use me however you choose."

My mom was upset because we started going to the Baptist church instead of the Catholic church. She called her sister, the nun, to talk with her about it. My aunt, Sister Irene, asked her why she was so concerned. She expressed that we were serving the same God and that she should just let us go. My mom settled down after that. Thank God!

Three years later, I'm finishing Secretarial School and looking to the future for my career and life. My brother worked hard on it and managed to get Mike and me together. We really didn't date much. Our dates consisted of Mike coming to my parents' house with his guitar and spending time singing and worshiping God. After just a short few weeks, we both knew God had brought us together. Mike asked me to marry him, and five and a half months later, we were married. At this moment, as I write, we're about to hit 47 amazing years together!

You Don't Need Those Glasses Anymore, Just Put Them in a Drawer!

Then Jesus placed his hands on the man's eyes again, and his eyes were opened. His sight was completely restored, and he could see everything clearly.

— *Mark 8:25 NLT*

Mike and I were married in 1977, and it was the winter of 1979 when Mike was building an apartment for us to live in on the third floor of a friend's house. I was pregnant with our first child, and Mike was hurrying to get our new apartment finished before the baby was born.

It was almost 10:00 p.m., and Mike was building the stairs that led up to the third floor. He was nailing a piece of plywood, and the board kept bouncing so the nail wasn't going in. Mike got a little frustrated and took a quick, hard swing at the nail. He just caught the edge of the nail with his hammer, and it bounced off, and somehow the finish nail came loose and stuck in his left eye.

Mike shook his head and blinked. As he did, the nail fell out onto the floor, and several drops of liquid fell from his eye. When he opened his eyes again, it was like looking through wax paper from the left eye. He could see light, but nothing more. Oh no! I can't lose my sight in that eye, Mike thought, and, suddenly, he just began to lift his voice to God in worship.

His friend heard him singing and could tell something wasn't right and asked him what happened. Mike explained what had happened. He quickly called for an ambulance, and off Mike went to the hospital. They put Mike on a bed, and several interns took turns looking at Mike's eye. Apparently, not many people have eye injuries like this, so these interns were standing in line to get a look at the injury.

Finally, an ophthalmologist arrived and looked at Mike's eye as well. The nail had pierced the cornea and the iris, but other than that, it didn't appear to have caused significant damage that would require surgery. They decided that they would give him drops to prevent infection, bandage both eyes for several days, and then see how things were at the end of the week.

So Mike spent one week lying in bed with both eyes bandaged up and nothing to do but wait and pray. "God, let me see more than just an opaque, obscure image of light from my left eye. I want to see like I did before," was Mike's prayer.

Meanwhile, I am eight months pregnant with our first baby, and I'm an executive secretary in the osteopathic hospital in Portland, Maine, for the director of nursing. "If only Mike had been wearing his glasses, this never would have happened," I thought. So I took his glasses and got them repaired so that when he was out of the hospital, he would be able to wear them.

Mike remembers quite distinctly the first morning in the hospital after the accident. Both of his eyes were bandaged up so he couldn't see a thing, and breakfast had just arrived. He was in the wing where other eye patients from cataract surgery were. The nurse explained to Mike the food situation: "At 12 o'clock is your toast, 3 o'clock your eggs, 6 o'clock is your bacon, and 9 o'clock is your coffee." Then off she went, leaving Mike to fend for himself as he ate his breakfast.

Several of Mike's friends stopped by to visit him to help the week go by faster. Finally, Friday arrived, and the doctor came back to take off the bandages. Mike was elated when he realized all of the cloudiness had gone away and he could see clearly out of his left eye. Promptly, I handed Mike his glasses and said, "Put these on. If you had been wearing them, this never would have happened!"

Mike put on his glasses but quickly took them off. "These aren't my glasses! These are way too strong. They hurt my eyes." To which I replied, "Yes, they are. I took them in to get the bow replaced that was broken." Mike tried to wear them for 30 minutes or so, but they began to give him a headache, so he took them off and said, "I can't wear these." I said, "We are going to go to the eye doctor tomorrow and see what is going on."

When we went to the eye doctor the next day and we explained what had happened and now Mike's glasses are giving him headaches, the doctor gave Mike a thorough eye exam, and when he had finished, he said this to him: "Well, you now have 20/20 vision. You don't need these glasses anymore; just put them in a drawer!" Glory to God! And that is exactly what he did.

ANDREA DAVIS

Rescued From a Raging River

When you pass through the waters, I will be with you; and through the rivers, they shall not overflow you. When you walk through the fire, you shall not be burned, nor shall the flame scorch you.
— Isaiah 43:2 NKJV

I was driving home after work along with a friend around 1:00 a.m. and found myself in the middle of a torrential downpour. I had only lived in the area a short time and was unfamiliar with the roads and the danger that was just up ahead. The roads were dark, and there were no streetlights in the area. I was just a few miles from my home as I rounded the corner in the pitch-black darkness, and I saw a car coming toward me that had just passed some train tracks. The car was driving very slowly, but I thought nothing of it due to the weather conditions.

The road descended down into a recreational park area with picnic tables and a large stream on the other side of the train tracks, and I was somewhat blinded by the oncoming headlights. I didn't see that the stream had overflowed its banks and was now a raging river completely flooding the basin of the park. I was unaware that the fire department had been out there earlier in the evening blocking off the road with a barrier so no cars could pass through due to the flooding.

However, that was hours earlier, and the water levels had continued to rise, completely submerging the barrier. I didn't realize that the car that had just passed me had actually turned around due to the flooded roads. In a matter of seconds, I drove into the flooded roadway, and my car suddenly stalled, and I felt that we were no longer on the road but floating sideways. My roommate, who was also in the car with me, and I sat there for a few seconds trying to figure out what our plan was. Water began leaking into my car through the doors. Before we knew it, the floorboards were quickly filling up with water, and my car was caught up in the current of the river.

Panic quickly set in, and we were both screaming. My car started to rotate, and we were now moving backward down into the darkness. As the swift current was washing us downriver, we abruptly collided with a tree, stopping us. Meanwhile, water was continuing to pour into the car, filling it up, and we were now sitting completely submerged in icy cold water. As we looked out our car windows, miraculously, the water never reached the top of our doors, and somehow, we were floating!

As we realized that the car was now stationary and no longer moving, we decided to roll down the windows and crawl out and climb up and sit on the roof of my car and call for help. Fortunately, I had thought to grab my cell phone and keep it from being submerged in the floodwaters. My first call was to my brother, who was 4 hours away in Oklahoma, as I was living in Kansas City at the time. I quickly explained our dilemma, asked him to pray for us, and then tell me what I should do. He asked me if I had called 9-1-1. I hadn't, because I wanted my first call to be for prayer. So I quickly said goodbye and called 9-1-1 for help.

Fortunately, there was a fire department just a mile or two down the road. They responded in a matter of minutes, pulling up with their fire truck; however, getting us to safety was not that simple. The river was swollen, and the water levels kept rising, and we were stuck up against a tree down river. There was no easy way to access us. They decided they couldn't attempt to do a water rescue of this nature since it violated their safety protocols.

The city called in two more surrounding fire departments, and as each one arrived and investigated the circumstances, they each declined to attempt a water rescue for the same reasons. Meanwhile, as the clock kept ticking, we were trying to keep our hopes alive as we sat there on the top of my car, shivering in the heavy rain that was drenching us. Hypothermia began to overtake us.

Finally, a fourth company of the fire department arrived with a ladder truck, and this water rescue team agreed to perform a water rescue. Their first plan was to attempt a helicopter rescue, but due to where we were located under the trees and with the magnitude of the storm, they decided it was too risky. Their second attempt was to try and reach us using a boat, and two fire-fighters made it all the way to our car with the boat. However, as they attempted to get me into the boat, it got caught in the strong current of the river and began to sink as it took on water. So now there were four of us trapped out in the middle of this raging river.

Their only other option was to back up the ladder truck as close as they could and work on extending the ladder and getting a rope over to us. Once they got the rope over to us, one of the fire-fighters tied it to a tree. Suddenly, we heard the sound of a train approaching! The rescue team had notified authorities that they were performing a water rescue in close proximity to the train crossing, and they were supposed to delay any trains from coming into the area until the rescue was over. However, this train was unaware of the rescue, and they blew the usual warning sounds using the train whistle as the train came barreling through. The fire truck was parked just a few yards off the tracks when the train drove past, narrowly missing hitting the firetruck and avoiding a major catastrophe.

Continuing the water rescue, next they sent their strongest firefighter, who has performed strongman competitions, to pull himself through the water as he was attached to the security rope so he could reach us. Then they had me lay on an inflatable raft, and he had to pull me over to the fire truck as he fought against the current of the river. The current of the river was so strong that it was lifting up the part of the fire truck that was submerged in the water, and they were in fear of losing their truck.

Once I was safely on the other side, they had to lift me up and help me crawl to the front part of the fire truck and then lower me down to get in the ambulance. Now, the rescue team went back and did the same rescue mission for my roommate and brought her to safety. Once we were in the ambulance, we were hooked up to monitors, and they covered us with heated blankets, and they turned on heated fans to warm us up.

We had been exposed to the elements and icy-cold waters for several hours, and we were suffering from hypothermia. I later found out I was minutes away from going into cardiac arrest due to the severe hypothermia my body had endured. The firefighters had seen me slowly getting worse and worse while we waited to be rescued. Later, they told me they were very concerned I was not going to make it, and when they saw how fast I started to decline sitting in the half-sunken boat, they told the rescue team on land, "We have to move fast with her." I shook for hours after being rescued, and it took me days to finally feel warm again.

The next day, I woke up to our story being all over the news and radio stations. I had news stations calling me for interviews! I felt overwhelmed with all of the attention after going through the most dangerous event in my life. I went to see my car the next day, and where the road had flooded, I saw how my car was nose-down, leaning up against the tree that had snagged us. I was confused at first because we had been sitting on the roof of my car... how could it be angled like this, and yet we sat on it for hours?

What I found out was the water levels had been so high and the current so strong that my car was suspended in ten feet of water. The only thing that kept my roommate and me from floating down the river was the tree my car got stuck on! I knew then that God sent His angels to hold our car up as we were trapped in the current of the raging river, and they protected us from what could have been a very different tragic ending. Thank you, Lord, for loving me so much you would reach down from Heaven and save my life!

Pastor Santiago

A faithful man shall abound with blessings....
— *Proverbs 28:20 KJV*

On September 16, 1985, my father was murdered. I was 13 years old. A man had been shot on the other side of our village, and the rumor spread that someone with the last name Miranda had killed that person. So one of the sons of that father grabbed a rifle and set off to shoot the first Miranda that he saw. As he passed by our house, he shot and killed my father.

I grew up in a small farming village. My family was very poor. We were a large family with ten brothers and sisters between us. In my childhood, I never owned a store-bought toy or new clothes. I didn't even own a pair of shoes until I graduated from the 5th grade.

Two years later, in 1987, my brother Matias was shot in an ambush. He was returning from working in the fields and was riding in the back of a pick-up truck with several other workers, all with the last name Miranda. Suddenly, there was a shot from the nearby mountain that hit Matias. It took several weeks for him to recover, and during that time, my family decided to travel to Acapulco and stay with a relative to get away from the village for a few weeks. Soon, we learned that in our absence, several of my uncles had taken over the property. So we couldn't return to live in the village where we grew up. We couldn't even return home!

We didn't have any money, so our large family was all crowded into a one-room apartment with no services. Later, we moved into a small house on the edge of the mountains. However, there was no security, and people stole what little we owned. Finally, my older sister was able to find an apartment in a nice area, so we all moved in with her.

My life after moving to Acapulco was filled with work in the morning, followed by studies in the afternoon, and then more work at night. There were times that I ended up working until 4 a.m., just to have to get up in a few hours to start my regular morning work routine.

I had received the basic Catholic teaching growing up, and from time to time, I would go to a church service. However, I never felt fulfillment or peace in my heart from God. At the age of 13, I got drunk for the first time in my life, and I often went to parties, bars, or discos.

My older sister and her husband were living in Cancun, Mexico and after receiving Christ into their lives, they felt compelled to share their experience with our entire family. So they traveled all the way to Acapulco, and after telling us of their experience, they brought us to a Christian church service (Llamados Para Servir) where we could hear the Gospel message of Jesus Christ.

After the service was over, she introduced our entire family to the pastors of the church (which included Mike and Kim Davis) with this message: We recently became Christians and want you to share the Gospel with my family and invite them to accept Jesus in their hearts and have them come to your church. So they shared the Gospel message with us, and we all prayed with them.

After meeting and praying with the American missionaries, Mike and Kim Davis, we began going to their church services. My mother and several of my brothers immediately made a commitment to follow Christ. My mother and sister were involved in Mexican witchcraft that descended from ancient Indian culture, and they stopped practicing witchcraft from that moment on.

However, I didn't want anything to do with this "following Christ" thing. My life was filled with hurt and bitterness, and I would argue with my sister and mother when they tried to talk to me about their new experience with Christ. I told them both that I didn't want to hear about it, that I was fine the way I was, and I would just continue being a Catholic.

In early January of 1994, I was sick with a fever for almost a week. While I was in bed, my brother Herbito gave me a Bible and several brochures called Chick Tracts. I read several of them, not letting anyone see me, because I was not in agreement with all the changes I was seeing in my family. While I lay in bed, I also read the entire book of Revelation in the Bible and was amazed by what I had read.

Days later, another missionary, along with Mike Davis, organized baptisms, and my mother invited me to go to the river with them. After begging me several times, I finally agreed to go. However, I went resentfully, as I was full of anger. I didn't want anything to do with the Gospel. I even told my mother that I would go, but I would find something else to do when I got there.

When we were riding on the bus, on the way to the river, they were singing praises to God and playing the guitar. I thought everyone was crazy. At one point I tried to get off the bus, but something stopped me. I sat down again.

Upon arriving at the Papagayo River, I was already making my getaway plans. However, I didn't do anything because I decided I didn't want to be rude. I stayed and listened to the message, and right there, as we were all huddled together on the riverbank, I accepted Christ in my heart. It felt as if someone raised my hand for me! Suddenly, a burden was lifted off from my life, and a beautiful feeling was born inside me.

I had such a strong conviction and decision to follow Christ that as they explained what Baptism was all about, I decided to get baptized right then. I understood that I was born again and a new creature in Christ. From that moment on, I have been living for Him. It all began on Sunday, January 16, 1994.

In April of 1994, three months after accepting Christ, I woke up startled by a dream at 4:00 a.m. I immediately began to pray. My mother and brothers woke up because they heard me praying, and they joined in. Suddenly, the Lord baptized me in the Holy Spirit, and I began to pray in other tongues! It felt so beautiful that I prayed in the Spirit until 6:00 a.m.

From that date, the change that God made in me was radical. He removed the desire to do the things that I did before. I never drank again. I have kept faithful to God and live a life of holiness, and I have never turned back! I went to college for four years and earned a degree in accounting and today I am the accountant and legal representative for the ministry that brought me to Christ under Apostles Mike and Kim Davis.

I began to serve the Lord by helping clean the church on Sundays. Later I served as an usher, and then I taught in the children's department for a long time. God completely transformed my life!

You've already read my story "Stop, I want you to pray for me!" where the Lord performed a miracle and sent me to plant a new church in the village of El Tamarindo in 2005, a town about four hours down the Costa Chica de Guerrero, doing work as missionaries with my wife and my two children. Currently, I am also the pastor of the church in Puerto Marques, the first church that was planted after the city-wide crusade back in 1987. To God be the glory!

Pastor Rafa

*Praise ye the Lord. Praise God in his sanctuary: praise him
in the firmament of his power. Praise him for his mighty acts:
praise him according to his excellent greatness. Praise him with
the sound of the trumpet: praise him with the psaltery and harp.
Praise him with the timbrel and dance: praise him with stringed
instruments and organs. Praise him upon the loud cymbals:
praise him upon the high sounding cymbals. Let everything that
hath breath praise the Lord. Praise ye the Lord.*
— *Psalm 150 KJV*

Like most Mexican families, I grew up in a Catholic home. We never really went to church or even practiced the faith. As for school, I dropped out at the age of 12.

During that time, my older brothers were learning to play music. They started a band called the Aces of Rhythm, and from the first moment I heard them playing, I knew I had to play as well. The strongest desire to play music was born in me. Every time they practiced, I was there watching, listening, learning, absorbing.

As days turned into weeks, and weeks into months, the love for music grew steadily within me. I studiously watched how they arranged music using different chords and notes. I understood music intuitively, thereby saving my brothers the burden of having to teach me. I could pick up any instrument and play it. Looking back, I can see that God gave me this gift, and eventually it would be used for the sake of the Gospel.

I was just fourteen years old when my brothers invited me to fill in for their absentee drummer. I started on drums but then began filling in on keys, lead guitar, and bass. I took advantage of every opportunity offered, and I began to advance quickly. I became skilled in every instrument, as well as on vocals.

At that point, other groups began recognizing my talent. They started inviting me to play in their bands. Eventually, I separated from my brothers.

At age fifteen, I joined a group called Youth Reborn. We played under contract in many local bars, parties, and even recorded music. Things were really starting to take off!

At sixteen, I got a big break playing with the Legends of Acapulco. We were well known, performing in many venues, recording several projects, and I started making a lot of money.

As you can imagine, my hedonistic lifestyle, like many worldly musicians, was full of vices. This lifestyle, along with the countless late nights, was wearing me down. One morning after a grueling succession of late-night gigs, I had an unexpected conversation with my brother and cousin, in which they informed me that they had both become born-again Christians. I guess I looked pretty bad to them—I was definitely feeling pretty bad at the moment—because they seemed very concerned about me.

Even though I thought I was living the dream, playing in nightclubs, recording music, and making a lot of money at the age of eighteen, my life was really a wreck. So, naturally, I told them I was doing great. I lied.

They invited me to a church meeting at Llamados Para Servir, AR, but I told them I wasn't interested. After that, we went our separate ways. Sometime later, they came to me again and invited me to church. Now, feeling even more haggard and empty inside, I knew something had to change. So I agreed and went along with them.

The people there were very friendly and welcoming. The pastor preached his message, and it seemed like his every word was directed straight at me. It was like he had been reading my mail! Then he gave an invitation to come forward and accept Christ, and I couldn't resist. What a change that came over me! The deep void I had felt inside all of my life was at long last filled!

When I wasn't playing in clubs, I attended more church services. One day, the pastor asked me if I would like to join the music ministry and play for the church. At the time, I still had five contracts to fulfill. I eventually completed four of those contracts before making a complete break with that life. I stopped smoking, drinking, and using drugs. I stopped with all the nightclubs and nightlife. That's when my life significantly changed for the better.

I took charge of the musicians and music ministry of the church and later was invited to preach. We did a lot of outreach events where music and preaching were involved. We held outreaches everywhere we could: from parks to basketball courts, anywhere we could preach openly and invite people to receive Christ as their Savior.

A few times, I was invited to hold evangelistic crusades in the Cancun area by the missions director. I brought our music ministry with me, and we held open-air concerts, followed by the preaching of the Gospel, then ministry for healing and salvation.

We were busy planting churches in the suburbs on the other side of the mountain from Acapulco. At the time, we had eight local churches spread out around the city, resulting from so many people receiving Christ in the evangelistic crusades we were conducting.

Currently, I am the music director and lead pastor of three churches, as well as the Vice President of Llamados Para Servir, AR. All to the glory of God!

Pastor Carlos

Even as [in His love] He chose us [actually picked us out for Himself as His own] in Christ before the foundation of the world, that we should be holy (consecrated and set apart for Him) and blameless in His sight, even above reproach, before Him in love.
— *Ephesians 1:4 AMPC*

I was born on February 12, 1974, the same day my father was killed. The details of my father's death aren't completely known, even to this day, other than there was a dispute between my family and another in the village. That and the fact that he was shot and killed at 5:00 p.m., and I was born four hours later at 9:00 p.m.

I was then left in the care of my grandparents as my mother fled for her life. She took my two older brothers and older sister with her, leaving me behind. When I reached the age of five, she returned for me. She had managed to build a small house for us all to live in.

Growing up I suffered from epilepsy. The doctors gave me medication to try and control the disease, but I would often fall down in severe convulsions that were uncontrollable. At sixteen years old, I returned to the village that my mother originally fled from, our home village, Axoxuca, where one of my uncles was the pastor of a church. I attended one of his services and answered his altar call for healing at the end of the service. I went forward and was immediately and completely healed! I gave my heart to Christ and have never suffered from any sign of epilepsy since!

From that day on, I was on fire for God. I joined the Davis' church in Puerto Marques and soon became their youth leader. At the age of nineteen, I was ordained as pastor of a house church in Tres Palos.

One day, as I was on my way to hold a church service, the Lord spoke to me about purchasing land to build a church. I did have some money saved up to purchase a keyboard for the music ministry, but I felt impressed by the Lord that the money was for the land instead. I called Apostles Mike and Kim, being under their ministry, and I wanted to make sure I wasn't making a mistake. They encouraged me to do exactly what the Lord had said.

I already knew of the perfect place to build the new church, and it would cost $30,000 pesos to purchase the new property. After speaking with Apostles Mike and Kim, they came up with the plan that their end of the ministry would raise $15,000 pesos, and that on my end of the ministry, we would raise the same.

I arrived at church for service, and that day there were some first-time visitors from Canada. After service, they came and struck up a conversation with me. They told me where they were from and that they were led by the Lord to attend our church that morning. Afterward, she handed me $15,000 pesos and told me to let them know if there was anything else they could do to help us build this church!

I could hardly wait to call and tell Apostles Mike and Kim that God had supplied every peso we needed! It was time to buy and start building. We quickly purchased the property for the new church in Tres Palos and now we are ready to break ground and start building the new church!

I began to seek the Lord about the construction of the new church building. He gave me a plan and design for the new church sanctuary and parsonage. I had limited experience in construction but felt the Lord's hand was on me to build this new church.

Putting together a small work crew, we began by building a perimeter wall around the property about 5 feet high. The plot of land was in a flood zone, and we needed to elevate the entire parcel of land. We had dump truck after dump truck come and back fill the area until it was level with the new perimeter walls.

The new church was to be constructed using steel reinforced concrete since we are in an earthquake zone. We dug the foundation for each new concrete column 3' x 3' x 3' and set the steel rebar for the columns in place and poured the concrete in the foundation holes we had dug for the new columns. Once all the columns for the exterior walls were completed, we built the new walls using solid concrete blocks.

The design the Lord gave me for the new roof was metal girders welded together with metal panels on top. I hired a man who lived in our neighborhood to weld the metal structures together. I watched him weld the first metal structures together and then he handed me the welder and said, "You can weld the next one." So, I did!

Once the new church sanctuary was completed, we built the parsonage where my family and I were to live and then we held a special inauguration service and dedicated the new church to the Lord.

A few years later the Lord spoke to us about starting a Bible Institute to train up new pastors and leaders. We built a new 2 story structure on the property in front the church for the Bible Institute.

We also host an annual weeklong youth conference, so I am building a 3rd story on top of the Bible Institute to serve as a dormitory.

God's vision is often so much larger than ours! I never dreamed that when I was first pastoring the house church that God had all of this in His heart. My wife Irene and I are eager to see what still lies ahead in the future.

It All Started With a City-Wide Crusade in Acapulco

And Jesus came and spoke to them, saying, 'All authority has been given to Me in heaven and on earth. Go therefore and make disciples of all the nations, baptizing them in the name of the Father and of the Son and of the Holy Spirit, teaching them to observe all things that I have commanded you; and lo, I am with you always, even to the end of the age.' Amen.
— Matthew 28:18-20

In November of 1987, several ministries from the United States all came together to host a city-wide crusade in Acapulco, Mexico. The speakers included Richard Roberts, Billy Joe Daugherty, Morris Cerullo, Sandy Brown, along with KSEA Ministries that brought down a crew of 168 people to help work the city-wide event. KSEA Ministries was the same group that originally invited us to take part in the medical missions on our first mission trip.

There were 2 main events that happened simultaneously during the Acapulco crusade. There were meetings being held in downtown Acapulco at the convention center, and open-air crusades on the other side of the mountain from the city of Acapulco. Hundreds of people attended each of the events and countless numbers accepted Christ as their Savior.

One of the venues that was very successful on the other side of the mountain from Acapulco was held at a basketball court in Puerto Marques, and many villagers attended the evening crusades and accepted Christ.

One night after the event was over, the Lord spoke to the director of KSEA Ministries and said, "I'm holding you responsible for all of the souls that have accepted me as their Savior." As a result, he purchased a property in Puerto Marques and a new church was planted. This happened in several other locations as well during the week-long event, and in the end, 4 new churches were planted altogether.

We arrived on the scene 2 years later and helped plant the new church in Tres Palos. Then, 2 years later when the director of the organization stepped down, we transitioned into the leadership position and Davis World Missions, Inc. was founded and continues today.

We invite you to prayerfully consider partnering with us as we continue this work in Mexico. At the release of this book, we have thirty-five years dedicated to the mission field along with: 7 churches, 4 full-time pastors, a Bible school, 3 annual mission trips with continual outreaches, and we are just getting started! Praise God!

The more support we receive, the more we can do to make a difference in these precious people's lives; the more miracles—just like the ones in this book—will continue to take place.

When you partner with us, you are the ones making it happen! God will be using you to fund the Great Commission, which means you will also be sharing in the harvest! That's a win-win scenario for everyone!

THE GOSPEL IS THE POWER OF GOD

For I am not ashamed of the gospel of Christ: for it is the power of God unto salvation to every one that believeth....
— Romans 1:16 KJV

The Gospel is the power of God released in our lives through a personal relationship with God's son, Jesus Christ. Jesus came to set the captives free! Whatever has kept you in a prison of darkness, Jesus has the keys to unlock the door of your captivity and set you free!

What is Good News to someone who is sick? They don't have to be sick anymore!

What is Good News to someone who is poor? They don't have to be poor anymore!

What is Good News to those in bondage? Jesus has come to set you free!

What is Good News to the broken-hearted? Jesus has come to heal your brokenness and fill you with joy!

What is Good News to those who are fearful? Fear not! For Jesus is with us always!

The Spirit of God, the Master, is on me because God anointed me. He sent me to preach good news to the poor, heal the heartbroken, announce freedom to all captives, pardon all prisoners. God sent me to announce the year of his grace—a celebration of Gods' destruction of our enemies—and to comfort all who mourn, to care for the needs of all who mourn in Zion, give them bouquets of roses instead of ashes, messages of joy instead of news of doom, a praising heart instead of a languid spirit. Rename them "Oaks of Righteousness" planted by God to display his glory.
— Isaiah 61:1-3 MSG

The Gospel is the story of God reaching down from Heaven with His supernatural power through Jesus Christ into our lives, saving us from the clutches of evil and the Kingdom of

Darkness. God is light, and in Him is no darkness at all! God is a good God and He has come to us with the Gospel message of Good News.

Maybe you have been held captive by fear. Fear is a force of darkness that holds you in bondage and keeps you from enjoying a life filled with joy and happiness. Fear is a crippling force that holds you in its grip, not allowing you to walk freely and enjoy life to its fullest.

The Good News is Jesus has come to set you free from the grip of fear. Jesus said, "Fear not! Only believe." When you have faith in Jesus Christ, fear has to flee! Faith conquers fear. Faith is a force, and the force of faith destroys fear. It reduces it to nothing. Fear has to flee in the presence of faith.

God sent His Son into the earth to demonstrate God's love and power. When you experience the fullness of the love of God in your heart, your life will never be the same. God is all-powerful and when His love fills your heart, His power overshadows you in such a way that fear has to flee!

God is love, and He is the Author of life. Jesus came to destroy the works of darkness. Sickness is a work of darkness, and Jesus was anointed by God and went about doing good and healing all who were sick and oppressed of the devil (see Acts 10:38). God is a good God, and the devil is a bad devil. Jesus is the healer! The Gospel is the power of God to heal every sickness and every disease. You don't have to be sick anymore!

Your Heavenly Father owns everything! All the fullness of earth belongs to Him, and you are His sons and daughters. Jesus became poor so that you might be made rich!

For you are recognizing [more clearly] the grace of our Lord Jesus Christ [His astonishing kindness, His generosity, His gracious favor], that though He was rich, yet for your sake He became poor, so that by His poverty you might become rich (abundantly blessed).
— 2 Corinthians 8:9 AMP

A good man leaveth an inheritance to his children's children:

76

and the wealth of the sinner is laid up for the just.
— Proverbs 13:22 KJV

If a good man will leave an inheritance to his children's children, wouldn't a good God leave an inheritance to His children? Absolutely, without a doubt! God has made a way for you and me as His children to flourish and prosper as we live for Him.

The Word of God is the will of God for your life. Whatever you see in Scripture, God is declaring to you as His desire for your life.

...I am come that they might have life, and that they might have it more abundantly.
— John 10:10 KJV

But my God shall supply all your need according to his riches in glory by Christ Jesus.
— Philippians 4:19 KJV

Beloved, I pray that you may prosper in all things and be in health, just as your soul prospers.
— 3 John 2 NKJV

You shall remember the Lord your God, for it is He who gives you power to get wealth, that He may confirm His covenant that He swore to your fathers, as it is this day.
— Deuteronomy 8:18 ESV

...I am the Lord your God, who teaches you to profit, who leads you in the way you should go.
— Isaiah 48:17 ESV

The steadfast love of the Lord never ceases; His mercies never come to an end.
— Lamentations 3:22 ESV

He heals the brokenhearted and binds up their wounds.
— Psalm 147:3 ESV

So how do we experience the healing love and mercy of God? We simply take God at His Word, and we invite Him into our lives.

We invite you to make this declaration of faith to God:

God, I believe that you are a God of love, mercy, and kindness. I believe you sent Jesus to die on the cross of Calvary for my sins. He took my place on that cross and paid the penalty for my sin.

Jesus, I ask you to come into my life, forgive me of all my sins, and fill me with your healing love. Fill the empty void in my heart with your Holy Spirit of love, joy, and peace. Wash away every hurtful thought and replace it with a new revelation of your great love for me. I choose to replace those memories with your Word and your promises for my life.

If this was the first time you prayed the prayer of faith asking Jesus to come into your life, you just received eternal life, and your name was written in the Lamb's Book of Life! If this was the first time you prayed, we would love to know. You can contact us by going to our website at: Davisworldmissions.com and sharing with us your story!

That Christ may dwell in your hearts through faith; that you, being rooted and grounded in love, may be able to comprehend with all the saints what is the width and length and depth and height—to know the love of Christ which passes knowledge; that you may be filled with all the fullness of God.
— Ephesians 3:17-19 NKJV

Yet in all these things we are more than conquerors through Him who loved us. For I am persuaded that neither death nor life, nor angels nor principalities nor powers, nor things present nor things to come, nor height nor depth, nor any other created thing, shall be able to separate us from the love of God which is in Christ Jesus our Lord.
— Romans 8:37-39 NKJV

WE INVITE YOU TO CONSIDER PARTNERING WITH US!

...Everyone who calls on the name of the Lord will be saved.' But how can they call on him to save them unless they believe in him? And how can they believe in him if they have never heard about him? And how can they hear about him unless someone tells them? And how will anyone go and tell them without being sent? That is why the Scriptures say, 'How beautiful are the feet of messengers who bring good news!'
— Romans 10:13-15 NLT

When it comes to missions, there are senders and there are goers! Oswald J. Smith once said, "You can either go on a mission trip or send a substitute."

When the Lord first called us to be missionaries to Mexico, we realized quickly we couldn't go without partners. We began the process of calling up pastors at every church we could and asked them for the opportunity to speak in their church with the hope that God would speak to someone's heart to partner with us.

We invite you to pray and consider partnering with us so we can bring the Gospel message of Jesus to Mexico and continue building and planting new churches and expand the Kingdom of God!

To become a partner and make a donation, you can visit our website at Davisworldmissions.com or donate via PayPal: Davisworld-missons@gmail.com.

You can also send a donation to our address at: Davis World Missions, P. O. Box 453 Bixby, Oklahoma 74008

WE BUILD CHURCHES!

Our ministry has been reaching out to the poorest villages in the area through medical clinics and open-air evangelistic crusades. We follow up with those who have accepted Christ by visiting them in their homes, and then we plant a new church in their village. Over the past 30-plus years, we have built six new churches, and we are currently in the process of building the seventh one in Las Lomitas.

Below is our sixth church in the mountain village of El Tamarindo, where there are only about 85 houses. Most everyone works as a farmer, and several are indigenous Indians who speak dialects as well as Spanish.

IGLESIA CRISTIANA
LLAMADOS PARA SERVIR, A.R.

**LLAMADOS PARA SERVIR A. R.
RENACIMIENTO, ACAPULCO, GRO.**

PASTORS RAFA AND MARY

**LLAMADOS PARA SERVIR A. R.
TRES PALOS, ACAPULCO, GRO.**

PASTORS CARLOS AND IRENE

**LLAMADOS PARA SERVIR A. R.
LLANO LARGO, ACAPULCO, GRO.**

PASTORS RAFA AND MARY

**LLAMADOS PARA SERVIR A. R.
PUERTO MARQUEZ, ACAPULCO, GRO.**

PASTORS SANTIAGO AND ANALIS

**LLAMADOS PARA SERVIR A. R.
COL. DEL PRI, ACAPULCO, GRO.**

PASTORS NOLBERTO AND AIDA

**ALONG WITH OUR MINISTRY IN
MEXICO, LLAMADOS PARA SERVIR,
WE HAVE BEEN BUILDING THESE
CHURCHES OVER THE PAST
30 YEARS!**

FIND US ON FACEBOOK!

FACEBOOK.COM/LLAMADOSPARASERVIRACAPULCO

LAS LOMITAS

We are in the process of constructing our seventh church in the village of Las Lomitas, a community that includes indigenous people who speak both a local dialect and Spanish.

During our recent mission trip in July, we had the opportunity to visit several families in their homes, and their joy at our presence was heartwarming. Their houses, made of simple sticks and featuring dirt floors, are located in the hills outside the village.

One of the dedicated members of the church, Mary, is just 35 years old and already has 13 children along with several grandchildren!

www.ingramcontent.com/pod-product-compliance
Lightning Source LLC
Chambersburg PA
CBHW051235120626
46547CB00013B/1650

* 9 7 9 8 9 8 7 8 9 6 9 7 6 *